THE UNOFFICIAL
2002
WORLD CUP
REFEREES
JOKE
BOOK

First published in Great Britain by
The Chicken House, 2, Palmer Street,
Frome, Somerset BA11 IDS

Text by Michael Powell
© The Chicken House 2002
Cover and inside illustrations © Paul Daviz 2002
Cover design by Alison Withey
Designed and typeset by Dorchester Typesetting Group Ltd
Printed and bound in Great Britain

ISBN 1 903434 22 X

Contents

THE SECOND HALF

Introduction

IT'S OFFICIAL: this unofficial joke book is the most awesome collection of football howlers you will ever read. It's got enough dynamite in its shorts to make other joke books look like a huge jar of marmalade.

Football is not just about scoring goals – it's about having a really good laugh. If you can't laugh, what's the point in getting out of bed at the end of the day? As Thierry Henry famously said: 'Sometimes in football you have to score goals.' And sometimes you have to roll around on the centre line giggling and gasping for breath.

So who better to show you the silly side of World Cup football than the man who has been the butt of more jokes than David Beckham hasn't understood: the REFEREE!

Have you ever wondered what the bald man in black shorts writes in that little notebook of his? Do you wish you could lip-read when he's giving the players a good talking to? Well now you don't have to, because we've stolen his book!

That's right! Here for the first time are the jokes that professional referees have for generations passed around and swapped with players and linesmen during top international fixtures.

Is it any wonder that Stuart Pearce missed that penalty in the 1994 World Cup quarter-final? He was still trying to keep a straight face after hearing the classic gag:

Why are football players never asked for dinner?
Because they're always dribbling!

It wasn't easy getting hold of these jokes, because a referee is taught 'to keep those things up his sleeve, close to his chest'.

But when a team is nil–nil down, the referee is there to help them see the funny side, because in the words of Tony Adams: *'Left alone with our own heads on, we can be pretty mental.'*

Reading this book is just like playing a game of footy. Laugh your socks off until half-time (the middle of the book!). Then enjoy some locker room laughs before kicking off into the second half.

Not only are all the best football jokes in the world right here, you can 'Ask the Anorak' about football trivia, there are lots of Own Goals (silly quotes), quizzes, the low-down on the 32 qualifying countries and teams, and even some cool games you can play while watching the World Cup on telly.

Make this book a must-have part of your World Cup 2002 experience. A bacon sandwich of a read if ever there was one!

6

The First Half

The History of Football (yawn!)

So when did the great and noble game of football begin?
Here's a quick history, cutting out all the boring bits, of
course . . .

The first historical report for football appears in China,
in the writing of the Han Dynasty about 2000 years ago.

The Romans played a game called *Harpastum* in which two
teams faced each other across a central line. The ball
was thrown in and each team tried to get the ball across
a line at the other end.

Ball games in Britain started as huge annual events in
which the whole village would compete. Two teams of
unlimited numbers started in the market-place and tried
to get a ball (usually a pig's bladder) into the opposite
side's goal at either end of the town. A mass fight kicked
off as teams used brute force and extreme violence
against each other. People who lived along the route
barricaded their windows for protection. Players were
lucky if they ended the day without being seriously
injured, but anyone managing to score became a
superhero!

The game grew in popularity until in 1314 Edward II banned
it in London, 'as there is great noise in the city caused by
hustling over large balls'. Later kings also tried to stop

8

'such idle practices'. By the time of Elizabeth I, football was stronger than ever, but it was still just a big fight, with no rules or referees and lots of injuries and even deaths.

A few rules appeared in Cornwall in the seventeenth century, but it wasn't until 1846 that the Cambridge Rules were created, and in 1863 they became the basis for the Football Association Rules we use today. It was only now that it was officially against the rules to pick up the ball. Also one of these rules stated: 'No player shall be allowed to wear projecting nails or iron plates . . . on the soles or heels of his boots.' Yikes!

Even though FIFA was formed in 1904, it took them almost thirty years to create a true international competition for professionals. There was the Olympics, but that was (and still is) for amateurs. Lots of top 'professional' teams had to drop out of the 1928 Olympics for this reason. But FIFA and the International Olympic Committee couldn't agree on who should control the Olympic soccer tournament.

Finally FIFA announced that it was *their* ball, so *they* would decide who could play or not! And so they set up the Jules Rimet Cup, claiming to be the biggest soccer event in the world.

Nowadays, host countries have to prepare for ten years for the big event, but in May 1929, FIFA still had not decided who was going to host the first championship in 1930. Uruguay ended up as hosts after everyone else dropped out. They went on to win the first World Cup final – and the rest, as they say . . . is football.

9

THROW-IN

Three ways a referee can improve his eyesight:

1 *Only look at things that are close to him.*
2 *Go to bed with a carrot under his pillow.*
3 *Wear his contact lenses.*

Kick-off

What has a head, a tail, but no body?
A coin.

Why did the chickens get sent off during the World Cup final?
For fowl play!

Why can't Cinderella play football?
She keeps running away from the ball.

Why can't skeletons play football?
They don't have the guts.

There were two muffins watching the World Cup final. The first muffin says, 'This is a really exciting game' and the second muffin says, 'O MY GOD, IT'S A TALKING MUFFIN!'

Why wouldn't the oyster pass the ball?
Because it was a little shellfish.

It's half-time and England are being hammered 4–1 by
Croatia. Sven-Goran Eriksson is giving the England team
a roasting in the locker room.
'Everyone who thinks they're stupid, please stand up!'
After three minutes of embarrassed silence Michael
Owen finally gets to his feet. Sven asks 'So why do you
think you're stupid?'
'I don't,' said Michael. 'I just hate seeing you stand up
there all alone.'

Why did the David Beckham stare at the can of
apple-juice?
Because it said 'concentrate' on it.

Sol Campbell visits the team doctor with a carrot in his
nose, a cucumber in his left ear and a piece of cheese in
his right ear. Sol says, 'Doc, what's wrong with me, I have
a carrot in my nose and cucumber and Stilton in my ears!'
The doctor looks at him and says, 'You just haven't
been eating properly . . .'

What part a football stadium is never the same?
The changing rooms.

What did one flea say to the other after they left the match?
'Shall we walk back to our hotel or take a dog?'

What happens when cows play football?
They get creamed.

11

What's white and green and travels at 25 miles per hour?
Michael Owen's handkerchief.

What kind of umbrella does Francesco Totti carry when
it's raining?
A wet one.

What's purple, 10,000km long and 12m high?
The grape wall of China!

A man called Luis Figo
Dreamt he was eating his shoe
He woke up one night
With a terrible fright
To find it was perfectly true.

One day the team bus crashed with twenty members of
the Italian World Cup squad in it, and the police came to
do a head count. They counted twenty-four heads. Why?
Because they counted *twenty foreheads.*

A Brazilian fan had a really bad seat at a World Cup
qualifying match. Looking through his binoculars, he
spotted an empty seat near the front. Thinking 'what a
waste' he pushed through the crowd to the empty seat.
When he arrived, he asked the man sitting next to it, 'Is
this seat taken?'
The man replied, 'This was my wife's seat. She passed
away. She was a big Brazil fan.'
The other man replied, 'I'm sorry to hear that. Why
didn't you give the ticket to a friend or a relative?'
The man replied, 'They're all at the funeral.'

The Republic of Ireland are 3–1 down to Saudi Arabia in Stage One. At half-time the manager, Mick McCarthy does the unthinkable and substitutes Roy Keane for a centipede. Everyone thinks Mick is crazy to replace their best player with a small multi-limbed insect. But the centipede turns the game around and scores five goals and Ireland win 6–3. Roy Keane goes up to the centipede at the end of the match to congratulate his team mate. 'Why didn't Mick play you in the first half?' asks Roy. The centipede replies, 'It takes me 45 minutes to get my boots on.'

What do you call a Scotsman in the finals of the World Cup?
The referee.

What did the duck say when he bought World Cup tickets?
Put it on my bill please.

What animal would Italian defenders like to be on a cold day?
A little otter.

Posh: I can say the word 'goal' in 32 different languages!
Becks: That's amazing. Go on then.
Posh: The word goal in 32 different languages.

How can you divide six potatoes among 20 footballers?
Boil them and mash them!

13

What do you call the Italian World Cup squad at the North Pole?
Lost.

In what month do football players earn the least?
In February – it's the shortest month.

Becks: Do you file your nails?
Posh: No, David. When I cut them off, I throw them away.

What comes at the end of the World Cup?
The letter P.

THROW-IN

How does a team reach the championship game?

First, the thirty-two teams will be split into eight groups, with four teams in each group. Each team plays the other teams in its group. The top two teams from each group go through to the knockout stage, which begins on June 15. The two teams that survive the knockout rounds will meet in the championship game, scheduled to be held on June 30.

The Trophies

The French sculptor Abel Lafleur designed the first World Cup trophy, called the Jules Rimet Cup. This gold statuette weighed nearly 4kg and was about 35cm tall, representing 'winged victory' on an octagonal base. (It looks a bit like a mermaid with wings standing up and carrying a bird bath on her head.)

Unfortunately this famous trophy was stolen at an exhibition in London just before the 1966 World Cup, but it was soon discovered by a dog called Pickles under some bushes!

In 1930 it had been agreed that the first nation to win the trophy three times should keep it forever, so when Brazil won their third final in Mexico 1970, they got it for keeps. However, in 1983 it was stolen again, and has never been recovered.

The present trophy is called the FIFA World Cup. It weighs about 5kg, is 36cm tall and is made of solid gold and malachite. It appeared at World Cup 1974 (West Germany) and was made by the Italian sculptor Silvio Gazzaniga. This is how he described it:

> *'The lines spring out from the base, rising in spirals, stretching out to receive the world. From the remarkable dynamic tensions of the compact body of the sculpture rise the figures of two athletes at the stirring moment of victory.'*

For those of you who don't worship the great game, you can get the same effect by sticking a yellow tennis ball to a table with a huge wad of well-chewed bubble gum, then pulling the ball away to a height of 36cm!

This trophy cannot be won outright as the rules state that it shall remain FIFA's own property (for that read: 'These trophies are just too expensive to keep giving away to the South Americans. They'd only get it nicked again, anyway.') The World Cup winners keep it for four years and then exchange it for a gold-plated replica. Cheapskates!

THROW-IN

What does a referee keep in his pockets?

We chose a referee at random, tipped him upside down and shook him hard for five minutes. These are the items that fell out of his pockets.

1 Coin with 'heads' on both sides.
2 Picture of his mum.
3 Red and yellow cards.
4 Three pairs of contact lenses, never used.
5 Bottle of Brasso (for shining his bald head).
6 A greasy old comb with three hairs stuck to it (last used in 1994).
7 Six spare whistles and a mouldy apple core.
8 A wide-screen TV with surround sound and video recorder (to catch the action replays).
9 Marilyn Manson CD.
10 False teeth.
11 Chest wig.
12 Plane ticket to Brazil dated 1983.
13 The Jules Rimet Cup.

Who in the world are they?

There are 32 teams in the World Cup Finals. Here is the low-down on 16 of them. Check each country's Big Guns and Star Players, and learn some amazing facts! The other 16 teams are in the second half of this book.

CHINA

They have waited 44 years to qualify. This is their first time.

Big Guns: Li Weifeng, Hao Haidong, Qi Hong, Ma Mingyu, Sun Jihai, Li Tie.

17

Star Player: Fan Zhiyi, (defense, midfield, Dundee) d.o.b. 6.11.69.
In 1998 he became one of the first Chinese professional footballers to move to Europe when he joined Crystal Palace for a transfer fee of £1 million.

Did you know?

- ⚽ Coach Bora Milutinovic is the only man to coach four different World Cup teams into the second round.
- ⚽ One of those teams is Costa Rica, which is the first team China will play on June 4.
- ⚽ There is enough stone in the Great Wall of China to build an eight-foot wall around the equator.
- ⚽ China only has about 200 family names, despite a population of over a billion.
- ⚽ More people speak English in China than in the United States.

JAPAN

This is only their second final (they first qualified in 1998).

Big Guns: Philippe Troussier (coach), Junichi Inamoto (Arsenal), Shinji Ono (Feyenoord).

Star Player: Hidetoshi Nakata (striker, AC Parma) d.o.b. 22.01.77.
He's one of the best footballers in Asia. In 1998 he became the youngest Asian Footballer of the Year.

18

During WC98 he dyed his hair red. What will he do this time? In 2001 he signed a four-year contract with AC Parma for £18.5m. In Japan he's treated like a pop idol.

Did you know?

- ⚽ Japan qualified automatically as a 2002 World Cup co-host.
- ⚽ The team has never won a WC final match.
- ⚽ Japan is one of the most crowded countries in the world, with 330 people per square kilometre.
- ⚽ Many Japanese golfers carry hole-in-one insurance, because in Japan you have to send presents to all your friends if you get a hole-in-one.
- ⚽ In Japan, it's illegal to buy or eat rice grown in another country.

SOUTH KOREA

This is their sixth WC final (it's an Asian record – and they've achieved five in a row) but they have never reached the second round.

Big Guns: Guus Hiddink (coach), Seol Ki-Hyeon (Anderlecht), Dong Gook Lee, Hong Myung-bo, Yoo Sang-chul, Hwang Sun-hong.

Star Player: Ki Hyeon Seol (striker, Anderlecht) d.o.b. 08.01.79.

He's one of the few Koreans who has performed well in one of the world's top leagues.

Did you know?

- ⚽ South Korea qualified automatically as a 2002 World Cup co-host.
- ⚽ The team has never won a WC final match.
- ⚽ Dutch coach Guus Hiddink is the first non-Korean to coach the team at a WC final.
- ⚽ Seoul, the South Korean capital, just means 'the capital' in the Korean language.
- ⚽ The national dish is *pulgogi*, or 'fire beef'.

 ## SAUDI ARABIA

The Persian Gulf's top football nation and the first Arab nation to qualify for three WCs in a row.

Big Guns: Nawaf Al Temyat, Talal al-Meshal.

Star Player: Sami Al Jaber (Wolverhampton Wanderers) d.o.b. 11.12.72.

He's the first Saudi professional to play in English football.

Did you know?

- ⚽ Saudi Arabia scored 43 goals to qualify – more than any other country.
- ⚽ They have had eight coaches since 1996.
- ⚽ Their best performance is 12th place at World Cup 1994.

- Saudi Arabia uses the most after shave and perfume in the world.
- A Saudi Arabian women can get a divorce if her husband doesn't give her coffee.

CAMEROON

This is their fifth WC final, a record in Africa.

Big Guns: Samuel Eto' o, Lauren Etame Mayer, Marc Vivien Foe

Star Player: Patrick Mboma (AC Parma) d.o.b. 15.11.70.

He has a degree in Maths and was African Player of the Year 2000.

Did you know?

- Cameroon is the only African side to have reached the WC quarter-finals (Italy 90).
- In 2000 they won the African Cup of Nations and an Olympic gold at Sydney.
- A big weakness is their inconsistent coaching.
- The country got its name after the Portuguese arrived 1472 shouting 'Camarões, camarões!' in amazement at all the giant shrimps.
- There over 130 ethnic groups in the country, speaking dozens of languages.

21

NIGERIA

Nigeria has over 200 professional footballers worldwide and are Africa's best hope for WC success. But this time they are in a tough group and they are quite inconsistent.

Big Guns: Sunday Oliseh, Finidi George, Victor Nwankwo Kanu, Victor Agali, Celestine Babayaro.

Star Player: Augustine 'Jay-Jay' Okocha (midfielder, Paris St Germain) d.o.b. 14.08.73.
A great dribbler with tricks and lots of character.

Did you know?

- They reached the second round in 1994 and 1998.
- The 'Super Eagles' won the Olympic gold in Atlanta in 1996.
- Nigeria occupies 15% of Africa but has 56% of its people.
- Nigeria has many famous writers including the Nobel Prize Winner Wole Soyinka, and Ben Okri.
- Despite its oil reserves, corruption and civil war has made Nigeria one of the twenty poorest countries in the world.

SENEGAL

They have never qualified for a WC final before. Africa's new kids on the block will be the Jamaica of this WC – watch out Brazil!

Big Guns: Bruno Metsu (coach), Khalilou Fadida, Henri Camara, Ferdinand Coly.

Star Player: Elhadji Diouf (striker, Lens) d.o.b. 15.01.81.

He's very fast, nicknamed 'Serial Killer' by his fans, but he can be a bit of a one-man band.

Did you know?

- ⚽ They have the lowest FIFA ranking of the five African nations in the World Cup.
- ⚽ When Senegal qualified, the president Abdoulaye Wade cut short a state visit in Europe to fly home to celebrate.
- ⚽ They qualified top of their group.
- ⚽ On May 31 Senegal's game against France will be the first of the championship.
- ⚽ Senegal is at the westernmost tip of Africa.

 ## SOUTH AFRICA

The top-ranked African nation on the FIFA World Rankings.

Big Guns: Phil Masinga, Mark Fish, Sibusiso Zuma, Delron Buckley, Siyabonga Nomvete.

Star Player: Shaun Bartlett (Charlton Athletic) d.o.b. 31.10.72.

The team captain, Bartlett, has potential to be big in English football: he's very quick, good in the air and has superb ball-control.

Did you know?

- The team's nickname is 'Bafana Bafana' which means 'the boys' in Zulu.
- South Africa came second to Germany in the battle to host the 2006 World Cup finals.
- Nelson Mandela was held prisoner by the South African Apartheid regime on Robben Island for 27 years until his release on February 12 1990.
- Mandela was one of the guests at Shaun Bartlett's wedding.
- South Africa has more sheep than any of the other WC finalists.

TUNISIA

A young and determined team, with a 'nothing to lose' attitude.

Big Guns: Chokri El Ouaer (goalkeeper-captain), Zoubeir Baya, Sirajeddine Chihi , Hassen Gabsi, Ali Zitouni, Ziad Jaziri.

Star Player: Adel Sellimi (striker, Freiburg) d.o.b. 16.11.72.

A superstar in Tunisia, he has been capped over 70 times. Nantes fans nicknamed him 'The Lung' because of all the running he does!

Did you know?

- ✪ In Argentina in WC 1978, they became the first African country to win a WC match when they beat Mexico 3–1.
- ✪ This is their third WC final.
- ✪ Tunisia will host the 2004 Nations Cup finals.
- ✪ Some of the space-age sets from *Star Wars* were filmed there.
- ✪ Men wearing shorts are considered to be in their underwear.

 ## COSTA RICA

This is their second WC final.

Big Guns: Rolando Fonseca, Paulo Wanchope.

Star Player: Hernán Evaristo Medford Bryan (Necaxa) d.o.b. 23.05.68.

He's the symbol of Costa Rican football.

Did you know?

- ✪ In 1990, Costa Rica became the first Central American country to reach the second round.
- ✪ Costa Rica was named as the most improved FIFA team of 2001.
- ✪ Their nickname is the 'Ticos'.

- ⚽ Christopher Columbus named Costa Rica (the 'rich coast') in 1502.
- ⚽ It has more butterflies per square kilometre than anywhere else on earth.

MEXICO

Whatever they do they'll do it with style. This is their 13th WC final.

Big Guns: Claudio Suarez, Alberto Garcia Aspe, Francisco Palencia.

Star Player: Cuauhtémoc Blanco (striker, Real Valladolid) d.o.b. 17.01.73.

A power-house Mexican hero, his famous party piece is the 'Cuauhtémiña' (where he balances the ball on both feet and twists past opponents).

Did you know?

- ⚽ Their best result in a WC final is sixth place (1970 and 1986).
- ⚽ The team's nickname is the 'Tri-Colores'.
- ⚽ Every year, Mexico City sinks about 10 inches (it was built on a lake).
- ⚽ In New Mexico, over 11,000 people have visited a tortilla that has the face Jesus Christ burned into it.
- ⚽ Mexico introduced chocolate to the world.

26

USA

They came last in WC 1998, but manager Bruce Arena has now started to bring in players from all over the world.

Big Guns: Kasey Keller, Brad Friedel, Earnie Stewart, Chris Armas.

Star Player: Claudio Reyna (Glasgow Rangers) d.o.b. 22.07.73.

One of the most talented footballers in the US ever, he's the son of an Argentinean professional footballer.

Did you know?

- ⚽ They have appeared in seven WC tournaments (including the last four).
- ⚽ Their best WC performance was third place way back in 1930.
- ⚽ Football is the fastest growing sport for girls in the USA.
- ⚽ USA drinks more cola than any of the other WC finalists.
- ⚽ USA shreds seven thousand tons of worn-out currency every year.

27

ARGENTINA

With their 13th WC final they are looking for their third win. Almost everyone in the team is a top European club player.

Big Guns: Juan Sebastian Veron (Manchester United), Crespo (Lazio, Italy), Gonzalez (Valencia), Samuel (Roma), Gallardo (Monaco), Ayala (Valencia), Zanetti (Inter Milan), Ortega (River Plate), and Sorin (Cruzeiro), Juan Roman Riquelme, Javier Saviola (Barcelona), Andres D'Alessandro (River Plate)

Star Player: Gabriel Omar Batistuta (striker, AS Roma) d.o.b. 1.02.69.

One of the world's greatest strikers. In May 2000 he joined AS Roma for £22 million, then the second-largest transfer fee ever.

Did you know?

⚽ Midfielder Juan Sebastian Veron is known as *La Brujita* (the little witch) for the way he glides as if riding a broomstick. He also plays Quidditch!

⚽ Only beaten by Brazil in qualifying rounds.

⚽ World Cup champions in 1978 and 1986, and losing finalists in 1930 and 1990.

⚽ Gabriela Sabatini is a famous tennis player from Argentina.

⚽ The dance 'the tango' comes from Argentina.

28

BRAZIL

The gods of the World Cup, they are the only team to have played in all WCs and the only one to have won four times. But this time they only just qualified!

Big Guns: Marcos (Palmeiras), Cafú, Emerson (AS Roma), Lúcio (Bayern Leverkusen), Roque Júnior (AC Milan), Roberto Carlos (Real Madrid); Vampeta (Flamengo), Edilson (Flamengo), Ronaldo (FC Internazionale Milan), Romario (Vasco da Gama) and Denilson (Real Betis).

Star Player: Rivaldo Vitor Borba Ferreira (striker, FC Barcelona) d.o.b. 19.04.72.

He's one of the best players in the world and named World Footballer of the Year 1999. Football genius, but has been criticised as a selfish player.

Did you know?

- ⚽ They were WC champions in 1958, 1962, 1970 and 1994.
- ⚽ They have reached the championship final six times.
- ⚽ They have finished in the top five twelve times.
- ⚽ Their worst performance was way back in 1930 when they came 14th.
- ⚽ But they had a staggering six defeats during qualifying for WC 2002.

29

ECUADOR

They amazed the world by qualifying for the final for the first time ever with five straight wins! Another 'nothing to lose' side who could be a wild card.

Big Guns: Cevallos (Barcelona), Ulises De la Cruz (Hibernian), Guerron (Deportivo Quito), Hurtado (La Piedad, Mexico), Alex Aguinaga (Necaxa).

Star Player: Agustín Delgado (Southampton) d.o.b. 2.12.74.

Nickamed 'El Tín', he's one of the most feared strikers in South America and the first player from Ecuador to play in the English Premier League.

Did you know?

⚽ During qualifying they were down to 10 men when they came from behind to beat both Peru and Paraguay 2–1.

⚽ They jumped 33 places in the FIFA world rankings, from 71st to 38th.

⚽ The Galapagos Islands belong to Ecuador.

⚽ Quito, the capital, is 2850m (9350ft) above sea level.

⚽ The Cotopaxi Volcano in Equador is the highest active volcano in the world.

30

PARAGUAY

Has a tiny population of only five million and yet this is their second consecutive WC final. Credited by Argentina as the toughest team they played in qualifying. But their star goalie, Jose Luis Chilavert is suspended for the first two matches (for spitting at Brazil's Roberto Carlos during a qualifier). Oh dear!

Big Guns: Arce (Palmeiras, Brazil), Caniza (Santos Laguna, Mexico), Roque Santa Cruz (Bayern Munich).

Star Player: José Luis Chilavert (Racing Strasbourg) d.o.b. 27.07.65.

He's the bad boy folk hero of Paraguay and one of the top goalkeepers in the world. World Goalkeeper of the Year 1995 and 1997. He has scored over 50 goals because he takes killer penalties and free kicks, but his quick temper gets him into trouble (hence his suspension).

Did you know?

⚽ They have appeared in six WC championships.

⚽ Their best performance is ninth place in 1930.

⚽ Duelling is legal in Paraguay as long as both parties are blood donors.

⚽ A favourite dance in Paraguay is the bottle dance in which performers swing around with a jar on their head.

⚽ Writer PJ O'Rourke once famously said: 'Paraguay is nowhere and famous for nothing'.

31

THROW-IN

In 1966, Italy suffered a national disaster by being sent out of the World Cup by North Korea in the group stage. The team flew home to a secret destination to avoid the press, but they still didn't escape being pelted with rotten fruit at the airport by angry Italian fans!

Ask the Anorak

1 **What is the highest number of goals scored in one WC match?**
Eleven. Hungary 10 v El Salvador 1 (Spain 1982)

2 **What is the highest number of goals scored by one player in a match?**
Five. Oleg Salenko, Russia v Cameroon (USA 1994)

3 **What is the highest number of goals scored by one player in a tournament?**
Thirteen. Just Fontaine, France (Sweden 1958)

4 **Who was the oldest player ever?**
Roger Milla, Cameroon, age 42 years and 39 days (USA 1994)

5 Who has had the most consecutive defeats?
Nine. Mexico (1930–58)

6 What was the largest attendance?
203,500 in Rio de Janeiro, Brazil for the match
between Uruguay and Brazil in 1950.

7 What was the smallest attendance?
300, Rumania v Peru at Montevideo (Uruguay 1930)

**8 What is the highest number of sendings off by a
referee?**
Five. Joel Quiniou (France 1986–94)
Yep, he had a red card and wanted to see if it worked!

9 Who had the shortest finals career?
1 minute. Marcelo Trobbiani. Argentina v W Germany
(Mexico 1986)

10 Who was the youngest player?
Norman Whiteside, age 17 years and 42 days (Spain
1982)

**11 Which two players hold the record for World Cup
appearances?**
Lothar Mattheus and Diego Maradonna with twenty-
one.

**12 What was introduced for the first time in the
World Cup in Mexico in 1970?**
Substitutes and red and yellow cards.

33

THROW-IN

Three things a referee never says:

1 *Oops, yes you're right – that was a penalty.*
2 *I can see that.*
3 *Shall I tie my hair up today or not?*

Crazy Games

Make Up Your Own Match Statistics

Have you noticed how commentators always seem to have the most ridiculous statistics at their fingertips? They can tell you how many times a player has passed the ball, or how many goals they have scored in their career, etc. But don't take their word for it. Why not make up your own absurd statistics while watching a game!

Pick a player and see how many times he:

spits
clears his nose
argues with the referee
touches his hair
hugs another player

34

falls over
fakes an injury
runs backwards
does something stupid
heads the ball
loses possession
falls to his knees
points
shouts

Pick a parent and see how many times they:

scream/cheer/laugh/cry
jump off the sofa
act like the world's biggest expert on footy
criticize
say 'yes' or 'no'
tell you to be quiet!

Listen to the commentator and see how many silly sentences you can spot. For example:

'Without the ball, he is a different player.'

'What that situation really needed was a little eyebrows.'

'Xavier, who looks just like Zeus, not that I have any idea what Zeus looks like . . .'

'It's going to take a shoehorn to prise these two teams apart.'

'It's only the absence of a goal we're waiting for.'

'The crowd think that Todd handled the ball . . . they must have seen something that nobody else did.'

'Scholes hits the goalpost – he could hardly have hit that any better.'

Three things a goalkeeper never says:

1 Can you reach that for me?
2 It's warm today, isn't it?
3 Hold this for me.

Early Doors

In a World Cup semi-final the capacity crowd watched a rather short striker running towards the goal looking dangerous.
He was immediately tackled by three large defenders who all hit him with a sliding tackle at the same time.
Regaining consciousness a few moments later, he looked round at the crowd and gasped,
'How did they all get back in their seats so quickly?'

Roy Keane was shown the red card for fighting.
Returning to the locker room, he had a terrible arm. It was covered in cuts and bruises and had a massive gash at the top, but he had no idea whose it was.

Striker: I had an open goal but still I didn't score. I could kick myself.
Manager: Don't bother. You'd only miss.

Zidane goes to a sports shop and asks, 'What are your football boots made with?'
The shopkeeper replies, 'Hide.'
Zidane says, 'Why should I?'
'No, no,' says the shopkeeper. 'Hide, hide: a cow's outside.'
'You can,' says Zidane, 'I'm not afraid of a cow.'

Why was Cinderella so bad at football?
Because her coach was a pumpkin.

Why is a leaking tap a good midfielder?
Because it is always dribbling but never gets out of breath.

A rather stupid fan arrives at a football match midway through the second half.
'What's the score?' he asks his friend as he sits down.
'Nil-nil,' comes the reply.
'And what was the score at half-time?' he asks.

First fan: 'I wish I'd brought the fridge to the stadium.'
Second fan: 'Why's that?'
First fan: 'Because I left the tickets on it.'

Why do footballers play better on Saturdays and Sundays?
Because all the other days are weak days.

Where do spiders play football?
Webley Stadium.

Michael Owen dies and enters the Pearly Gates. God takes him on a tour. He shows Michael a little two-bedroomed house with a faded Liverpool FC banner hanging from the front porch. 'This is your house, Michael. Most people don't get their own houses up here,' God says.
Michael Owen looks at the house, then turns around and looks at the one sitting on top of the hill. It's a huge four-storey mansion with white marble columns and a new Ferrari parked outside. Manchester United banners hang on both sides of the pavement and a huge picture of David Beckham sits in the front window.
'Thanks for the house, God, but let me ask you a question. I get this little two-bedroomed house with a faded banner and David Beckham gets a mansion with flags flying all over the place. Why is that?'
God looks at him seriously for a moment, then with a smile, says, 'That's not David's house, it's mine.'

What happened when Robbie Fowler slept under his car?
He woke up oily next morning.

38

Own Goals

'If that had gone in, it would have been a goal.'
DAVID COLEMAN

'It was one of the best goals I've seen this Millennium.'
TONY GUBBA

'The Italians are hoping for an Italian victory.'
DAVID COLEMAN

'It's headed away by John Clark, using his head.'
DEREK RAE

'Lukic saved with his foot, which is all part of the goalkeeper's arm.'
BARRY DAVIES

'52,000 here tonight, but it sounds like 50,000.'
BRYON BUTLER

'The ball was literally glued to the back of his foot – into the back of the net.'
ALAN PARRY

'Four minutes to go . . . four long minutes . . . three hundred and sixty seconds . . .'
ALISTAIR ALEXANDER

THROW-IN

In April 2001, a Brazilian referee hid in his locker room under police protection for an hour after sending off seven players. He was later given a police escort out of town.

Fantasy World Cup Squads

BRAZILIAN SQUAD FOR WORLD CUP 2002

Solo

Ditto

Memento   Psycho   Vimto   Tango

Cheerio   Subbuteo

SuperMario   Bono   Marilynmunro

SUBS
Nescafe Brasso Polio Piano Expo

40

CROATIAN SQUAD FOR WORLD CUP 2002

Itch

Annoyingitch   Scratchtheitch   Hardtoreachitch

Itchovitch   Brassic

Carinaditch   Eatyourspinach   Crossstitch

Ostrich   Ostrichovitch

SUBS
Muddypitch

RUSSIAN SQUAD FOR WORLD CUP 2002

Kickov

Ticlycov   Throaticov   Chesticov

Showof   Smirnof

Blastof   Chernobyl   Fallingof

Sendhimov   Ackny

SUBS
Stalin Benolin Rubitov Keepmeoff

41

ENGLAND SQUAD FOR WORLD CUP 2002

Iwantmymam

Poundoflamb   Firemansam

Beckham   Reckham   Kickham   Sackham

Pushapram   Flimflam   Whatasham   Rasberryjam

SUBS
Rackoflamb Tony Blair

SWEDISH SQUAD FOR WORLD CUP 2002

Ikea

Shelvingssen   Newsofassen   Wardrobessen

Bootsson   Shortsson

Ulrikajonsson   Jeremyclarjksohn

Secondcoussen   Thirdcoussen   Leftjawlitesson

SUBS
Onthebenchsson Stillonthebenchsson

I Want to be a Referee . . .

So you think you've got what it takes to be a professional referee? But how well do you know the rules of football? Answer these twelve questions to see if you shape up. **Good luck!**

FIFA OFFICIAL REFEREE EXAMINATION PAPER

Name: Date:

Multiple choice. Time allowed for this examination: three weeks. Answer all the questions. Write clearly using black or blue ink. If you don't know the answer then guess. If you need to ask your friends, go to the toilet or hum noisily, that's OK too. Chewing gum, fizzy drinks and MP3 players may be used at all times.

1. What is the maximum width of the white lines on the football pitch?

a) 12cm.
b) 5cm.
c) 30cm.
d) 1 metre.

2. A flag post must be at least how high?

a) 1 metre.
b) 1.5 metres.

c) 3 metres.
d) 50 metres.

3. If the crossbar of one of the goals becomes displaced or broken what do you do?

a) Stop play until it has been repaired or replaced in position.
b) End the match.
c) Break the other one and resume play.
d) Phone your mum for advice.

4. What's the minimum number of players a team must have before the game can begin?

a) Eleven.
b) Seven.
c) One – the goalkeeper.
d) Two (including the goalkeeper).

5. Where must a substitute enter play?

a) At the halfway line.
b) In his own half.
c) On camera.
d) Wherever the substituted player leaves the pitch.

6. Can players wear jewellery during a match?

a) Yes, anything goes.
b) No.
c) Yes, as long as it is in their team colour.
d) Only diamond studs on their boots.

7. Which items are compulsory for all players?

a) Shinguards.
b) Handkerchief.
c) Shorts.
d) Sandwiches.

8. Can a goal be scored directly from a kick-off?

a) Yes.
b) No.
c) Only by accident.
d) Yes, but only during injury time.

9. Can a player commit an offside offence when receiving the ball directly from a throw-in?

a) No.
b) Yes.
c) Only if it is foggy.
d) Only if the referee has already given him a warning.

10. If the referee sees a player spitting at an opponent, what should he do?

a) Show him the yellow card.
b) Award a penalty.
c) Allow the other player to spit back.
d) Show him the red card.

11. If the ball hits the referee and goes into the goal, what happens?

a) It's not a goal. The player who kicked the ball is given a yellow card.
b) It's a goal.
c) It's not a goal. The player who kicked the ball is given a red card.
d) The referee bursts into tears.

12. If a player takes a penalty kick, the ball hits the crossbar and returns to the same player, who then scores. Is it a goal?

a) Yes, as long as the ball doesn't hit the ground first.
b) No. The ball must be touched by a second player before the kicker can touch it again.
c) Yes, as long as he uses his other foot.
d) It's the referee's choice whether to award a goal.

Answers

1. (a) The maximum width is 12cm. None of the other answers really make sense, do they? And who thought it was one metre? What were you thinking? Why not just paint the whole pitch white!

2. (b) 1.5 metres. Erm . . . 50 metres and you're kind of stopping aeroplanes!

3. (a) The referee stops play until the crossbar has been repaired. If a repair is not possible, the match is abandoned. (Crossbars were introduced in 1882. Before that, tape was stretched between the posts eight feet above the ground.) The 1994 World Cup quarter-final between Mexico and Bulgaria came to a halt when the Mexican goal collapsed under the weight of several players falling into the net!

4. (b) A match can't start if either team has less than seven players. (The rule was invented after Argentina hammered Scotland in a friendly in 1996 after only three Argentinian players bothered to turn up – only kidding!)

5. (a) A substitute only enters the field of play at the halfway line and during a stoppage in the match. (But he must check his hair first!)

6. (b) A player must not use equipment or wear anything which is dangerous to himself or another player (including any kind of jewellery).

7. (a) and (c) The basic compulsory equipment of a player is: a jersey or shirt, <u>shorts</u>, socks, <u>shinguards</u> and footwear.

8. (a) A goal may be scored directly from the kick-off, and it happens!

9. (a) There is no offside offence if a player receives the ball directly from a throw-in, goal kick or a corner kick.

47

10. (d) A player is sent off and shown the red card if he spits at an opponent or any other person. A direct free kick is awarded to the opposing team.

11. (b) The referee is part of the field of play and therefore the goal is allowed. Nobody is shown a yellow or red card, because no offence has been committed, although it could bring tears to the referee's eyes!

12. (b) The ball must be touched by a second player before the kicker can touch it again.

Referee Rating

12 You got them all correct! Oh dear, oh dear. You're just TOO perfect to be a referee! Have you considered playing for Manchester United instead?

8–11 At least you got a few wrong, so there's still hope. Why not have another go, only this time don't use any common sense. Just say the first answer that comes into your head!

5–7 Way to go! But I wouldn't shave your hair off just yet. Go back and figure out where you're going right, then do the opposite!

1–4 Oh, so close. Just imagine that your brain is like a goal net: full of holes!

0 Congratulations. You're absolutely clueless. There's nothing to stop you from putting on those black shorts and blowing your whistle. Now, all you have to do to become a professional referee is answer one more question incorrectly. Are you ready?

How many fingers am I holding up?

THROW-IN

The great England football manager Alf Ramsay ran out onto the pitch after England beat Argentina in the 1996 World Cup quarter-final to stop his players from swapping shirts. He is reported to have said, 'We don't swap shirts with animals!'

Own Goals

'And now we have the formalities over, we'll have the National Anthems.'

BRIAN MOORE

'At least it was a victory and at least we won.'

BOBBY MOORE

49

'If you stand still there is only one way to go, and that's backwards.'

PETER SHILTON

'The margin is very marginal.'

BOBBY ROBSON

'It slid away from his left boot which was poised with the trigger cocked.'

BARRY DAVIES

'I'll never play at Wembley again, unless I play at Wembley again.'

KEVIN KEEGAN

'I'd have to be superman to do some of the things I'm supposed to have done, I've been at six different places at six different times.'

GEORGE BEST

'I'm not going to make it a target but it's something to aim for.'

STEVE COPPELL

'We've got nothing to lose, and there's no point losing this game.'

BOBBY ROBSON

'Kicked wide of the goal with such precision.'

DES LYNAM

'I am a firm believer that if you score one goal the other team have to score two to win.'

HOWARD WILKINSON

Later Doors

David Beckham is renegotiating his contract with Manchester United.
'You'll get £80,000 a week to start,' says Alex Ferguson.
'Then, after six months you'll get £100,000 a week.'
'OK,' replies Becks, 'I'll come back in six months.'

Why does Fabien Barthez eat little bits of metal?
He likes to have a staple diet.

If it takes ten footballers half-an-hour to eat a ham, how long will it take twenty footballers to eat half a ham?
It depends upon whether they're professionals or 'am-a-chewers.

What did Mark Kinsella say when he accidentally burped during the World Cup final?
'Sorry, it was a freak hic!'

Did you know that Becks is so rich he has two swimming pools, one of which is empty?
It's for people who can't swim!

Posh went on a banana diet.
She didn't lose any weight, but she can't half climb trees well!

Damien Duff sat on a train chewing gum and staring vacantly into space, when suddenly an old woman sitting opposite said, It's no good you talking to me: I'm stone deaf.'

A FIFA official visits an England training session at night. The whole squad are kicking balls around except for Emile Heskey who is hanging from the roof of the stadium by one arm. 'What's Emile doing?' the FIFA official asks the coach. 'Oh, ignore him,' says the coach. 'He thinks he's a floodlight.' 'Well, why don't you tell him he isn't?' asks the official. 'What?' replies the coach,' and train in the dark?'

Posh: Why are you going around telling everyone I can't sing?
Becks: I'm sorry. I didn't know it was meant to be a secret!

Becks: I want a box of chocolates for Victoria.
Shop Assistant: Sorry, sir. We don't do swaps.

Posh: Whisper something sweet in my ear.
Becks: Double chocolate chip ice cream.

Tomasz Hajto is standing at a bus stop eating fish and chips. Next to him is a lady with her little dog, which gets very excited at the smell of the soccer ace's supper and starts whining and jumping up at him. 'Do you mind if I throw him a bit?' Tomasz asks the lady. 'Not at all,' she replies. *So he picks the dog up and throws it over a wall.*

Michael Owen takes back a pedigree puppy to Harrods, complaining that it made a mess all over his house. 'I thought you said it was house-trained,' he moans. 'So it is,' says the assistant. 'It won't go anywhere else.'

THROW-IN

Saudi Arabia are never going to win a World Cup final but in 1990 they managed to score two goals in the group stage. Each scorer received a Rolls Royce as a reward!

Mascot Mania

The first World Cup mascot appeared for the 1966 tournament in England, and each World Cup has had one since then. It's a really big deal thinking up the mascot and the name, because it must sum up the national character of the host nation, be cute and loveable, and be turned into merchandise — so that millions of people can buy cuddly toys, badges, hot water bottles, you name it!

The 2002 FIFA World Cup has three computer-generated mascots, called Ato, Nik and Kaz. Ato is the yellow one, Nik is blue and Kaz is purple. They are supposed to be energy particles in the atmosphere!

So what mascots have other countries dreamed up since 1966?

In 1966 the England mascot was a lion playing football called 'World Cup Willie'. The next three World Cups used cute chubby little boys called Juanito (Mexico 1970), Tip & Tap (West Germany 1974) and Gauchito (Argentina 1978). Then in 1982 Spain started a fruit and vegetable theme with a smiling orange called Naranjito, which Mexico continued in 1986 with a chilipepper called Pique. Then, disaster! The Italian 1990 mascot was a terrible sculpture thing made out of red, white and green blocks – definitely the worst mascot ever! So we returned to 'safe' animals again with Striker the smiling dog in USA (1994) and Footix the smiling cockerel in France 1998.

If you were running the FIFA World Cup 2002, what mascot would you choose and what would it be called?

Ask the Anorak

(The Anorak would like to thank www.thisdayinfootball.com)

Do goal posts always have to be painted white?

It is a little-known fact that though goal posts are always painted white, there is no rule that says they have to be. In theory you could paint them any colour you like.

Why isn't there any advertising on the goal posts or back of the net?

No kind of commercial advertising is allowed on the field of play and field equipment (including the goal nets, flag posts or their flags).

What are the top ten silliest names in International Football?

Segal Richard Bastard (1880)
Harry Butler Daft (1889–92)
Alfred Henry Strange (1930–4)
Pelham George Von Donop (1873–5)
Herod Ruddlesdin (1904–5)
Rupert Renorden Sandilands (1892–6)
George Jacob Tweedy (1937)
Ernest Blenkinsop (1928–33)
Ernald Oak Scattergood (1913)
David Batty (1991–8)

Why is the ball round?

Have you ever tried heading a cube?

THROW-IN

When Italian player Fernando d'Ercoli, playing for Pianta against Arpax in 1989, was given the red card, he got so angry that he snatched it from the referee's hand and swallowed it!

Referee Jokes

Did you hear about the referee who had three pairs of glasses?
One pair for indoors, one pair for outdoors, and one pair for looking for the other two.

What happened to the stupid referee who put his false teeth in the wrong way round?
He ate himself.

What is the first thing a referee does in the morning?
He wakes up.

What do you call a referee who's black and blue all over?
Bruce.

What do you call a referee who lies on the floor?
Matt.

What do you call a referee lying in the gutter?
Dwayne.

What do you call a referee who has been dead and buried for thousands of years?
Pete.

What kinds of referees have their eyes closest together?
The smallest ones.

56

What would happen if you threw lots of eggs at a referee?
He would be egg-sterminated.

Referee: Doctor, doctor, I'm moulting. I need something to keep my hair in.
Doctor: How about a matchbox.

Referee: Doctor, Doctor, I snore so loudly I keep myself awake!
Doctor: Sleep in another room then.

What goes whistle, whistle, squelch, squelch?
A referee in soggy shoes.

How do you make a referee float?
You take two scoops of ice cream, a glass of coke and one referee!

When a referee falls into a pond, what is the first thing that he does?
Gets wet!

Now you see it, now you don't, now you see it, now you don't – what are you watching?
A referee walking over a zebra crossing!

What do you call a referee with a plank on his head?
Edward.

What do you call a referee with a car on his head?
Jack.

57

What do you call a referee with a seagull on his head?
Cliff.

What do you call a referee with a crane on his head?
Derek.

What do you call a referee with a wig?
Aaron.

What do you call a French referee with cat scratches on his head?
Claude.

What do you call a referee who forgets to put his underpants on?
Nicholas.

What do you call a referee who wears tissue paper shorts?
Russell.

How did the referee stop a cold from going to his chest?
He tied a knot in his neck.

Have you heard of the referee who is so short-sighted he can't get to sleep unless he counts elephants?

Why was the referee annoyed when he bumped into an old friend?
They were both driving their cars at the time.

58

Referee 1: What's that on your shoulder?
Referee 2: That's Tiny.
Referee 1: Looks like a reptile to me.
Referee 2: Yeah. He's my newt!

Referee 1: I've got a wonder watch. It was very cheap.
Referee 2: What's a wonder watch?
Referee 1: Every time I look at it, I wonder if it's still working.

Did you hear about the referee who had a bath put in?
The plumber said, 'Would you like a plug for it?'
The referee replied, 'Oh, I didn't know it was electric.'

Policeman: What gear were you in at the time of the accident?
Referee: Oh, the usual: black shirt, black shorts.

What's the difference between a referee and a kilo of lard.
One's a fat lot of good and the other is a good lot of fat.

Why did the referee decide to become an electrician?
To get a bit of light relief.

Did you hear about the vain referee who was going bald?
The doctor couldn't do a hair transplant for him, so he shrunk his head to fit his hair.

What has two heads, three hands, two noses and five whistles?
A referee with spare parts.

Referee: I want a haircut please.
Barber: Certainly, sir. Which one?

Referee: Can you give me something for my baldness?
Doctor: How about this skunk potion?
Referee: Will it make my hair grow back?
Doctor: No, but if you spray it all over your body, nobody will come near enough to notice that you're bald!

What's black and whistles in circles?
A referee in a washing machine!

What's black and whistles with 16 wheels?
A referee on roller skates!

Teacher: How do you spell referee?
Girl: R-e-f-f-e-r-r-e-e-e
Teacher: That's not how the dictionary spells it.
Girl: You didn't ask me how the dictionary spells it!

Why did the referee turn round every time his dog barked?
It said 'ref ref'.

How do you get a referee into a matchbox?
Take all the matches out first!

What does an agnostic dyslexic insomniac referee do at night?
He lies awake and wonders if there really is a dog!

Why did the referee bring toilet paper to the birthday party?
Because he was a party pooper!

60

Why did the stupid referee hit his head against the wall?
Because it felt so good when he stopped!

How many referees does it take to screw in a light bulb?
Three. One to hold the bulb, and two to turn the chair!

How do you confuse a referee?
Put him in a round room and tell him to sit in the corner!

How can you tell when a referee has been using the computer?
There is correction fluid all over the screen!

An exhausted looking referee dragged himself in to the Doctor's office. 'Doctor, there are dogs all over my neighbourhood. They bark all day and all night, and I can't get a wink of sleep.'
'I have good news for you,' the doctor replied. 'Here are some new sleeping pills that work like a dream. A few of these and your troubles will be over.'
'Great,' the referee answered, 'I'll try anything.'
A few weeks later the referee returned, looking worse than ever.
'Doc, your idea is rubbish. I'm more tired than before!'
'I don't understand it, said the doctor, shaking his head. 'Those are my strongest pills!'
'That may be true,' answered the referee wearily, 'but I'm still up all night chasing dogs and when I finally catch one it's impossible getting it to swallow the pill!'

What's the difference between an interfering referee and someone who's just got out of the bath?
One is rude and nosey, the other is nude and rosy.

What has a whistle and two wheels?
A referee doing a wheely on a skateboard.

What has eight legs and can't hold a tune?
Four tone-deaf referees carol singing.

THROW-IN

German referee Bayram Kaymacki was ruthless. But one day, he went just a bit too far! He red carded Osbert Vorwerk, who refused to leave the pitch. The referee, cool as you like, produced a gun and shot Osbert in the head. The bullet only grazed the player's ear, but his team-mates refused to play on until the referee was replaced. Afterwards Kaymacki told reporters, 'One has to maintain discipline on the field, otherwise the game doesn't flow properly and children can't enjoy it.'

Crazy Games

World Cup Bingo

Why not liven up a boring first round fixture with this World Cup 2002 Bingo Game! There are a hundred words below. Write them on pieces of paper and get each player choose ten at random and copy them onto their scorecards. If the commentators use one of your words, cross it off your scorecard. The first person to cross off all their words (or who has crossed off the most at the final whistle) is the winner.

ability
ambition
atmosphere
attack
bench
breathtaking
build
calibre
campaign
cap
captain
career
celebration

challenge
champion
chance
coach
combination
confident
consecutive
consistent
contender
contract
courage
creative
debut

defeat
defender
disappoint
disaster
dream
experience
famous
fans
fit
flank
flexibility
follow in the footsteps

football
foreign
giant
glory
goal
hat-trick
heart
hero
history
in the world
injury
international
leader

legend
line-up
lose
midfield
million
mistake
nation
net
off side
on paper
pace
partnership
pedigree

performance
physical
player
playmaker
popular
prayer
presence
proud
qualified
quality
record
recover
retire

season
shoot
skill
squad
star
striker
strong
style
surprise
talent
temperament
tense
threat

timing
transfer
trophy
unbeaten
underestimate
veteran
weakness
wild card
win
world-class
young player

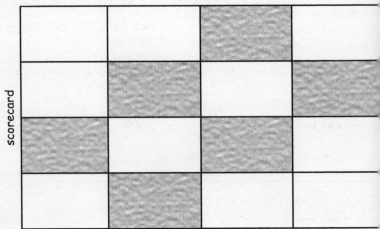

scorecard

Own Goals

'Our fans have been branded with the same brush.'
RON ATKINSON

'It will be a shame if either side lose, and that applies to both sides.'
JOCK BROWN

'Believe it or not, goals can change a game.'
MIKE CHANNON

'That would have been a goal if the goalkeeper hadn't saved it.'
KEVIN KEEGAN

'Apart from their goals, Norway haven't scored.'
TERRY VENABLES

'That's lifted the crowd up into the air.'
BARRY DAVIES

'Chile have three options – they could win or they could lose.'
KEVIN KEEGAN

'Zidane is not very happy, because he's suffering from the wind.'
BIG RON

Anagramantics

Did you know that if you rearrange the letters of the England coach, Sven-Goran Eriksson you get the sentence 'Sane governor sinks!' or that World Cup Football becomes 'Follow cup, drab lot!'

Anagrams are hilarious. Look what happens when you rearrange the letters of these great International players.

Roy Keane
No ear key

Emile Heskey
He like me? Yes
Eyes like mesh

Marcel Desailly
Calmly realised
Dear! Silly camel
Clearly mislead
Really calm side

David Beckham
Hived mad back

Ashley Cole
Solely ache
Hello Casey!

Alessandro del Piero
Deplored on salaries
Poser and ideal loser
Is a poodle slanderer

Rio Ferdinand
Friend in road
Finer android
Fodder in rain
Do in infra-red

Michael Owen
Now I'm a leech
Hi low menace
Whole cinema
How nice male
Whale income
Ahem! Nice owl
I chew a lemon

Alvaro Recoba
A brave car loo
A love or a crab
Alcove or a bra

Robbie Fowler
Borrow belief
Fibre or bowel?
Fire lower, Bob!

Henrik Larsson
Renal horn skis
Skin rash loner

Sol Campbell
Compels ball!
Male slob plc.

Zinédine Zidane
I ended in Zanze

Oliver Kahn
Oh! evil rank
OK rival hen

Shaun Bartlett
Resultant bath
The brutal ants
But rash talent
That table runs

And finally, here is a retired football legend:

Diego Maradona
An adored amigo

Injury Time

How do the Brazilian World Cup squad change a light bulb?
They hold it in the air, and the world revolves around them.

What tea does Gareth Southgate drink?
Penaltea!

Where do footballers dance?
At a football!

What did the bumble bee striker say?
Hive scored!

Half-Time Locker Room Laughs

What part of a football pitch smells nicest?
The scenter spot!

How did the football pitch end up as triangle?
Somebody took a corner!

What are Brazilian fans called?
Brazil nuts!

Why is it that birds are quickly sold when they come up on the transfer market?
They tend to go cheep!

What do you get if you drop a piano on a team's defence?
A flat back four!

What should a football team do if the pitch is flooded?
Bring on their subs!

What happens to a footballer when his eyesight starts to fail?
He becomes a referee.

Brazil are playing England in the World Cup final and are so confident of winning that they let Rivaldo take on the whole England team single-handed, while they put their feet up and watch it on TV. The match starts and the Brazilians celebrate as Rivaldo scores in the eighth minute to give Brazil a 1–0 lead. They turn off the radio and begin to celebrate and then turn on again near the end of the game. They are amazed to find that England has equalized in the 85th minute. They race to the stadium to help Rivaldo win the match, but they get stuck in traffic and arrive late to find the game over and the final score 2–1. Rivaldo is sobbing in the locker room.
"What went wrong?" they ask.
"I got sent off 2 minutes into the second half!"

When fish play football, who is the captain?
The team's kipper!

Brooklyn: My dad's David Beckham. He's got a great car –
it's red, flashy and goes really fast.
Friend: So has my dad: he's a fireman!

Why is David Seaman like dracula?
Because he hates crosses!

What is the best diet for wingers?
Runner beans!

What is French, 305 metres high and wobbly?
The Trifle Tower.

69

What nationality are you?
Well, my mother was born in Iceland and my father was born in Cuba, so I suppose that makes me an ice cube!

England are trailing by three goals when David Beckham gets knocked out after a dangerous tackle. After five minutes he finally regains consciousness. The team doctor is standing over him looking worried. 'Who am I?' Becks asks the doctor, clearly concussed. 'You're Pele' replies the Doc. 'Now get back on that pitch and score some goals!'

Sven: Why didn't you stop the ball?
David Seaman: What do you think the nets are for?

The Second Half

ENTRANCE EXAM FOR REFEREES PART II

Time Limit: 3 weeks

Name: _____

1. What language is spoken in Italy?

2. What must a referee remember to bring with him on to the pitch?
a) A whistle.
b) Red card and yellow card.
c) Notebook and pencil.
d) Shorts.
e) All of the above.

3. What did you have for breakfast this morning?
a) Breakfast.
b) Can't remember.
c) Who, me?
d) A shower.

4. Metric conversion. How many feet is 0.0 metres?

5. Spell the following:

Fabien Barthez: _____

Roy Keane: _____

Paolo Maldini _____

(If this is too difficult, just draw a picture at the top of the next page)

6. Six kings of England have been called George, the last one was George the Sixth. Name the previous five.

7. Why do you want to be a referee?
a) Yes.
b) No.

8. What are door handles for?

9. What is the man with the whistle on a football pitch called?
a) The referee.
b) Nigel.
c) Next Tuesday.
d) Cheri Blair.

10. What shape is a ball?
a) Ball shaped.
b) Round.
c) Where?

11. Advanced maths: If you have three apples, how many apples do you have?

12. What colour is red?
a) Yellow.
b) Red.

THROW-IN

When West Germany met Austria in Spain 1982, everyone knew that the only result that would allow both these neighbouring countries into the second round was 1–0. Germany scored after ten minutes and since it was in neither team's interests to score again, the game practically ground to a halt. The Spanish crowd started booing and one German supporter was so disgusted that he burned his national flag on the terraces. The next day Algeria who were knocked out as a result, appealed to FIFA saying that the match was fixed. Their protest was rejected, but the rules were changed in 1986 to prevent a repetition of this scandalous performance.

Manager Jokes

A manager is talking to his team before a big game. 'Now come on lads,' he says, 'we need to win this so that I can raise the cash to buy some new players.'

A tight-fisted football manager walks into a hotel. *'How much for a room?'*

'Thirty pounds a night and extra if you have a room with a view.'
'What if I promise not to look out of the window?'

Why did the football manager call both his children Ed?
Because he figured that two Eds were better than one.

Did you hear about the football manager who believed in reincarnation? *In his will he left all his money to himself.*

My uncle must be the meanest football manager in the world. *He recently found a crutch – then he broke his leg so he could use it.*

A doctor had been attending a rich old manager for some time, but the old chap had not long to live. So the doctor advised his wealthy patient to put his affairs in order. 'Oh yes, I've done that,' said the old manager. 'I've only got to make a will. And do you know what I'm going to do with all my money? I'm going to leave it to the doctor who saves my life.'

Why do football managers keep their clothes in the fridge?
They like to have something cool to slip into in the evening.

What has handles and flies?
A football manager in a rubbish bin.

What do you call a football manager with a double-decker bus on his head?
The deceased!

What does a manager wear to a tea party?
A tea shirt.

Why did the football manager put bread in his shoes?
Because he had pigeon toes.

Do football managers snore?
Only when they're asleep.

Why did the football manager go out with a prune?
Because he couldn't find a date!

What kind of flower grows on a football manager's face?
Tulips!

Why do old football managers cover their mouths with
their hands when they sneeze?
To catch their false teeth.

Did you hear about the manager who dreamed he was
eating an enormous marshmallow?
When he woke up his pillow had disappeared.

Why did the football manager fix his bed to the
chandelier?
Because he was a light sleeper.

THROW-IN

Italian Coach Enzo Bearzot picked Paolo Rossi for the 1982 World Cup squad even though he had just finished a two-year suspension from football because of a bribery scandal. Rossi played four games without scoring or sparkling. The pressure was really on. Everyone thought that the coach was mad to let him play against favourites Brazil in the quarter-finals but he proved everyone wrong and went on to score a hat-trick. Then he scored both goals in the semi-final 2-0 win against Poland. When he scored the first goal in Italy's 3-1 win over West Germany in the championship final, Rossi became the top scorer in the tournament!

Who in the world are they?

 ## URUGUAY

Another tiny country that's mad about soccer, this is their tenth WC final.

Big Guns: Fabian Carini (Juventus FC), Paolo Montero (Juventus FC), Pablo Garcia (AC Milan), Dario Silva

(Malaga CF), Gonzalo De los Santos (Valencia CF).

Star Player: Alvaro Recoba (Venezia) d.o.b. 17.03.76. Nickamed 'El Chino', he has blossomed at AC Milan. Also banned for four months for having an illegal Italian passport. Whoops!

Did you know?

- ⚽ They have won the World Cup twice in 1930 and 1950.
- ⚽ This is their first final in twelve years.
- ⚽ Their nickname is the *'Celeste'*.
- ⚽ A small purple flower grows so well there that Uruguay is also called the Purple Land.
- ⚽ Uruguay has one of South America's highest standards of living.

BELGIUM

They are the first team ever to qualify for six World Cups in a row (not counting hosts and defending champions).

Big Guns: Marc Wilmots (Schalke 04), Glen de Boeck (Anderlecht), Walter Baseggio (Anderlecht).

Star Player: Emile Mpenza (striker, Schalke 04) d.o.b. 04.07.78.
When he joined FC Schalke 04 in 2000 for a record fee close to nine million euros, he was still almost unknown outside Belgium.

78

Did you know?

- This is their 11th World Cup final.
- Their best performance was 4th place in 1986.
- Their nickname is the 'Red Devils'.
- French speaking residents of Belgium are called Walloons.
- Agatha Christie's famous detective, Hercule Poirot, is Belgian.

CROATIA

In WC98 they finished in an amazing third place but have since tumbled down the world rankings, but as Goran Ivanisovic proved in Wimbledon 2001, you should never write off the Croatians!

Big Guns: Davor Suker, Mario Stanic (Chelsea), Igor Tudor (Juventus), Dario Simic (Inter Milan), Bosko Balaban (Aston Villa).

Star Player: Alen Boksic (Middlesbrough) d.o.b. 31.01.70.
He's one of the most successful Croatian professional footballers of recent years.

Did you know?

- WC98 was their first World Cup final appearance.
- Only two other countries have won the bronze medal

79

in their first tournament appearance – USA (1930) and Germany (1934).

⚽ Croatia conceded just two goals during qualifying, the fewest of any country.

⚽ Croat Goran Ivanisovic won Wimbledon 2001 after begging to be allowed to play.

⚽ Dalmatian dogs originate from the Dalmatian coast of Croatia.

DENMARK

Includes some of Europe's elite.

Big Guns: Thomas Sorensen (Sunderland goalkeeper), Jesper Gronkjaer (Chelsea), Thomas Helveg (AC Milan), Martin Jorgensen, John Dahl Tomasson (Feyenoord).

Star Player: Ebbe Sand (Schalke 04) d.o.b. 19.07.72. One of Denmark's greatest ever strikers. Recovered from cancer in 1998. A calm and intelligent all-rounder.

Did you know?

⚽ This is their third World Cup appearance.

⚽ In WC98 they reached the quarter-finals, but lost to Brazil.

⚽ They were European Champions in 1992.

⚽ Hans Christian Andersen was Danish.

⚽ When it's somebody's birthday, Danes fly a flag outside their window.

80

ENGLAND

Most of the team play for Manchester United and Liverpool. Sven-Goran Eriksson is the first foreign coach. He's looking to better their 1990 performance.

Big Guns: Sven-Goran Eriksson (coach), David Beckham (Manchester United), Emile Heskey (Liverpool), Robbie Fowler (Liverpool), Rio Ferdinand (Leeds United), Sol Campbell (Arsenal), Ashley Cole (Arsenal)

Star Player: Michael Owen (Liverpool) d.o.b. 14.12.79. In 1998 he became the youngest player to play for England. After his amazing WC98, AC Milan were rumoured to have offered him £30 million, but he's fiercely loyal to Liverpool. A very mature player whose immature ham strings often let him down.

Did you know?

⚽ This is their 11th World Cup.

⚽ They came fourth in 1990.

⚽ They reached the quarter-finals in 1954 and 1962.

⚽ They were World Cup champions in 1966.

⚽ Winston Churchill was born in a cloakroom during a dance.

81

FRANCE

The defending champions are top favourites, but with a possible weakness in central defence.

Big Guns: Roger Lemerre (coach), Mickaël Silvestre, Marcel Desailly, Fabien Barthez, Patrick Vieira, Thierry Henry, David Trezeguet.

Star Player: Zinédine Zidane (Real Madrid) d.o.b. 23.06.72. He learnt to play football in the back streets of Marseilles where he was discovered by a Cannes FC talent-scout at age 14. Real Madrid paid a record £47.2 million for him.

Did you know?

⚽ France qualified automatically as the defending World Cup champions.

⚽ Their nickname is 'Les Bleus'.

⚽ They came third in 1958 and 1986 and fourth in 1982.

⚽ France eats the most cheese per person in the world.

⚽ It is illegal to kiss on French railways.

GERMANY

Second only to Brazil in WC success, but have been in decline for the past decade since stars Lothar Matthäus, Jürgen Klinsmann and Rudi Völler retired.

Big Guns: Mehmet Scholl (Bayern Munich), Jens Jeremies, Michael Ballack (Bayer Leverkusen), Jens Nowotny (Bayer Leverkusen), Christian Wörns, Thomas Linke (Bayern Munich).

Star Player: Oliver Kahn (Bayern Munich) d.o.b. 15.7.69. The model of consistency. German footballer of the year 2000.

Did you know?

- ⚽ They have won the World Cup three times in 1954, 1974 and 1990.
- ⚽ They have lost in the final three times.
- ⚽ This is their 15th World Cup final.
- ⚽ One in three Germans is a member of a sports club.
- ⚽ Germany is Western Europe's richest and most highly populated nation.

 # REPUBLIC OF IRELAND

Jack Charlton worked miracles before passing the job to Mick McCarthy.

Big Guns: Mick McCarthy (manager), Damien Duff (Blackburn Rovers), Matt Holland (Ipswich), Mark Kinsella (Charlton), Mark Kennedy (Wolves), Robbie Keane (Leeds), Clinton Morrison (Crystal Palace).

Star Player: Roy Keane (Manchester United) 8.10.71. All-round midfielder with boundless energy. 'Spuds' has emerged from injury a calmer player and an inspirational captain.

83

Did you know?

- ☺ This is their third finals appearance.
- ☺ Their best performance is 9th place in 1990.
- ☺ They gave away just five goals in qualifying, the fourth-lowest in Europe.
- ☺ Saint Patrick was kidnapped at the age of 16 by pirates and sold into slavery in Ireland.
- ☺ There are more Irish people in America than in Ireland.

ITALY

They are strong contenders despite a weak qualifying performance.

Big Guns: Francesco Totti (Roma), Christian Vieri (Inter Milan), Alessandro Del Piero, Filippo Inzaghi.
Star Player: Paolo Maldini (AC Milan) d.o.b. 16.06.68. One of the world's greatest defenders, he has played for AC Milan since he was a boy. He has perfect timing and has a reputation for being very reliable and fair.

Did you know?

- ☺ This is their 15th finals appearance.
- ☺ They were champions in 1934, 1938 and 1982, and runners-up in 1994.
- ☺ Their nickname is '*La Nazionale*'.
- ☺ Mickey Mouse is known as *Topolino* in Italy.
- ☺ Italy drinks more wine than any other WC finalists.

84

POLAND

Used to be one of the best teams in the world, but since the glory years of the 1970s and early 1980s, Poland has been in big trouble.

Big Guns: Emmanuel Olisadebe, Arkadiusz Bak, Marcin Zewlakow, Tomasz Klos, Marek Kozminski.

Star Player: Tomasz Hajto (Schalke 04) d.o.b. 16.10.72.
Few players can throw the ball further than him (over 35 metres!) or get as many yellow cards (he got 16 in the 98–9 season). But he's still one of Poland's best defenders. His nickname is 'Gianni'(Versace) because he's a sharp dresser!

Did you know?

⚽ This is their first WC final since 1986.

⚽ Poland has finished third at the World Cup twice in 1974 and 1982.

⚽ They won Olympic gold in 1972.

⚽ Famous poles include Marie Curie, Frederick Chopin and Pope John Paul II.

⚽ Pope John Paul II is the most recognized person in the world.

PORTUGAL

At their third WC final, they need to beat their reputation of getting nowhere by playing beautiful football.

Big Guns: Antonio Oliveira (coach), Rui Costa (AC Milan),

Star Player: Luis Felipe Madeira Caeiro Figo (Real Madrid) d.o.b. 4.11.72.
A gritty street footballer. After Euro 2000 he transferred to Real Madrid for £40 million, signing a six-year contract that guarantees him earnings of more than £27 million, yet very down-to-earth in his private life. European Footballer of the Year 2000. FIFA World Footballer of the Year 2001.

Did you know?

- ⚽ They came third in 1966.
- ⚽ Their last WC final was way back in 1986.
- ⚽ It is one of Europe's smallest countries.
- ⚽ The drink 'port' comes from the Portuguese town of Porto.
- ⚽ There are over 170 million native speakers of Portuguese worldwide.

86

RUSSIA

Qualified top of their group, but they have had a tough journey since the end of the USSR.

Big Guns: Oleg Romantsev (coach, says he will quit if they don't get into the second round), Valeri Karpin, Vladimir Beschastnykh, Dmitri Khoklov, Alexandre Mostovoi.

Star Player: Viktor Onopko (defender, Real Oviedo) d.o.b. 14.10.69.
One of Russia's most experienced players.

Did you know?

- ⚽ This is their 9th WC finals.
- ⚽ Their best performance is 4th place in 1966.
- ⚽ They have reached the quarter-finals three times (1958, 1962, 1970).
- ⚽ Russia has more trees than the other WC finalists.
- ⚽ During the time of Peter the Great, there was a tax on beards.

SLOVENIA

With only 2 million inhabitants they have defied the odds thanks to their remarkable coach, but it all rests on the fitness of one injury-prone and temperamental star: Zlatko Zahovic.

Big Guns: Srecko Katanec (coach), Milenko Acimovic (M, Crevena Zvedza).

87

Star Player: Zlatko Zahovic (midfielder, Benfica) d.o.b. 01.02.72.
A cult figure in Slovenia, he's a genuine box-to-box player but temperamental.

Did you know?

- ☺ This is their first WC final appearance.
- ☺ Coach Srecko Katanec's name translates as 'lucky'.
- ☺ They were undefeated in qualifying.
- ☺ Slovenia's karst caves are home to a famously weird creature called the 'human fish' up to 30 cm long with no eyes or skin pigment.
- ☺ The 'human fish' is a big tourist attraction and even appears on Slovenian coins.

SPAIN

They have arguably the best domestic league in Europe but have never improved on fourth place in 1950. However a new coach is bringing back an attacking style that suits them better.

Big Guns: Jose Camacho (new coach), Ivan Helguera (Real Madrid), Juan Carlos Valeron (Deportivo La Coruña), Vicente Rodriguez (Valencia), Fernando Hierro, Josep Guardiola.

Star Player: Raul Gonzalez Blanco (Real Madrid) d.o.b. 27.06.77
At 17 he was the youngest player ever to play for Real Madrid. He is one of the top players in the world.

88

Did you know?

- ✪ This is their 11th WC finals.
- ✪ They reached the quarter-finals in 1986 and 1994.
- ✪ They were runners-up in Olympic Games 2000.
- ✪ Picasso's full name was: Pablo Diego Jose Francisco de Paula Juan Nepomuceno de los Remedios Cipriano de la Santisma Trinidad Ruiz y Picasso.
- ✪ Spain gave the world spinach.

SWEDEN

Qualified without losing a single game, albeit in an easy group. They make up for slight lack of creativity with discipline and teamwork.

Big Guns: Magnus Hedman (Coventry City), Patrik Andersson (Barcelona), Zlatan Ibrahimovic (Ajax Amsterdam), Christoffer Andersson (Helsingborgs IF), Håkan Mild, Pontus Kåmark (IFK Gothenburg), Teddy Lucic (AIK Solna).

Star Player: Henrik Larsson (Celtic) d.o.b. 20.09.71. One of the most dangerous strikers in Europe, he scored 16 goals in his first season at Celtic, although a calf injury almost ended his career in 1999.

Did you know?

- ✪ This is their 10th WC finals.
- ✪ They came second in 1958 and third in 1950 and 1994.

89

- They didn't qualify in 1998.
- Sweden drinks more milk and coffee than any of the other WC finalists.
- In Sweden, it's illegal for parents to insult or shame their children.

TURKEY

A decade of rebuilding has paid off. They could be the biggest test to Brazil in the first round.

Big Guns: Rüstü Reçber (goalie), Hakan Sas (M, Galatasaray), Alpay Ozalan (Aston Villa).

Star Player: Hakan Sükür (striker, Inter Milan) d.o.b. 01.09.71.
This ruthless all-rounder is easily the most popular player in Turkey.

Did you know?

- This is only their second appearance; the first was in 1954.
- They were quarter-finalists in the European Championship 2000.
- There are no turkeys in Turkey.
- Anyone caught drinking coffee in Turkey in the seventeenth century was executed.
- *Shish kebab* (skewer-grilled lamb) is a Turkish invention.

THROW-IN

Twenty ways to annoy your family while watching the World Cup Final

1   Reply to everything the commentator says with, 'that's what YOU think'.
2   Practise making fax and modem noises.
3   Jump up and shout 'goal' whenever you feel like it.
4   Hide all your dad's beer.
5   Try playing 'Can't Get You out of My Head' by opening your mouth and flicking your cheek with your finger. When nearly finished announce, 'No, wait I got the last bit wrong.' Then repeat.
6   Ask 'Why is he doing that?' every time the referee stops play.
7   Repeat everything the commentator says very quietly.
8   Ask for help with your homework.
9   Say 'Ow!' every time someone kicks the ball.
10 Pretend you are Jimmy Hill.
11 Keep shouting 'Come on Scotland!'
12 Throw toilet paper at the TV.
13 Chant 'Two-nil, two-nil, two-nil, two-nil...' when the score isn't two-nil.
14 Shine a torch at the TV if it's a night game.
15 Before the game, wipe some dog food on the TV, so your dog keeps licking the screen.
16 If you don't have a dog, wipe some beer on the TV so your dad keeps licking the screen.
17 Ask your dad why he isn't a professional footballer.
18 Hide the remote control in your pocket and keep switching channels.
19 Take a photograph of the TV every time a goal is scored.
20 Sing 'Football's coming home...'

91

Match Munchies

Do you get the munchies when you're watching footy on the TV? In England we are famous for warm beer, black pudding and yeast spread, but what might viewers be munching in some of the other countries?

China: Bird's nest soup, bear paws, owl soup, fish flotation bladder.

Japan: Seaweed, *Fugu* (blowfish – deadly poisonous if cooked the wrong way).

Korea: *Kimch'i* – pickled cabbage dish (fermented mixture of vegetables, meat or fish, and very strong chilli peppers, pickled and sometimes buried in the ground), silk worm grubs, tiger parts soup.

Nigeria: *Durian* (fruit that smells of old socks), *Isi-ewu* (goat head pepper soup).

Senegal: Grasshoppers.

Mexico: Tequila worms, ceviche (raw fish marinated in citrus juice), grasshoppers.

USA: Spam, chewing gum, peanut butter.

Argentina: *Morcillas* (blood sausages), mixed grills (*parrillada*) including tripe, intestines, udders – the lot.

Brazil *Gari* (grated cassava root).

Croatia: *Piroska*, a greasy cheese doughnut.

Denmark: Beer-Jelly, *Gamle Ole* (smelliest cheese in the world), *Rastefisk* (boiled rotting fish), *Skaerpekoed* (leg of sheep hung for about 3 months).

England: Warm beer, black pudding, yeast spread.

France: Snails, frog's legs, brains.

Germany: Curry wurst, *Bierkase* (strong-smelling cheese made with beer yeast).

Italy: Song birds, *Cibreo* (cockerel's combs).

Slovenia: A strong brandy called *zganje*.

Spain: *Criadillas*, prairie oysters.

Sweden: *Sylta* (meat made from boiled animal heads).

Turkey: *Raki*, an aniseed-flavoured grape brandy.

THROW-IN

Julio Iglesias used to play for Real Madrid.
Eddie Large used to play for Manchester City.
Des O'Connor used to play for Northampton Town.
Rod Stewart used to play for Brentford.

Crazy Games

The M&M World Cup

For this game you will need several packets of M&Ms!
Each person picks a player and writes the name on a
piece of paper. Each player picks a name out of a hat.
Each time your player does one of the things in the table
below, you gain or lose M&Ms. But you can't eat any until
the end of the game!

Player wins possession	Gain 1
Player loses possession	Lose 1
Player has free kick awarded against him	Lose 5
Player has penalty awarded against him	Lose 5
Player has free kick awarded for him	Gain 5
Player has penalty awarded for him	Gain 10
Player scores goal	Gain 15
Player scores hat-trick	Gain whole packet
Player offside	Lose 5

Player spits	Lose 2
Player shoots at goal	Gain 2
Player misses easy goal	Lose 3
Player scores own goal	Lose 20
Player fakes an injury	Lose 5
Commentator praises player	Gain 1
Commentator criticizes player	Lose 1
Player substituted	Lose 10 (and pick another player)
Player argues with referee	Lose 5
Player performs two-footed leap into the crowd	Lose 30
Player gets into a fight	Lose 15
Player slips over	Lose 1
Player yellow carded	Lose 10
Player red carded	Lose everything!

THROW-IN

In May 2001, the coach of Ecuador's national soccer team was shot in the thigh after excluding 19-year-old Dalo Bucaram, the son of the former president, from the team. The shot was fired by one of the Bucaram family bodyguards!

95

Own Goals

'Both sets of players are putting in the sort of effort you see from antelopes trekking across the Sahara to warmer climes.'

NICK BARNES

'. . . the sort of goal . . . that makes the hair stand up on your shoulders.'

NIALL QUINN

'Many supporters say that they wouldn't stand for all-seater stadia.'

GUY MICHELMORE

'A game is not won until it is lost.'

DAVID PLEAT

'I'm not disappointed – just disappointed.'

KEVIN KEEGAN

'The lads really ran their socks into the ground.'

ALEX FERGUSON

'Hagi could open a tin of beans with his left foot.'

RAY CLEMENCE

'We are now in the middle of the centre of the first half.'

DAVID PLEAT

More Anagramantics

Francesco Totti
On softer tactic
Soft coat cretin
Strict foot acne

Raul Gonzales
Alas! Zero lung
Goals run zeal
Zealous gnarl

Gabriel Batistuta
Alas! Big attribute
Artist albeit a bug
A big, suitable tart
Blast! Bite a guitar

Cuauhtémoc Blanco
Touch! A calm bounce
Am a cute, cool bunch
A much able coconut
Numb coach ace lout
O! Accountable chum

Claudio Reyna
I adore lunacy
Our daily acne
I a royal dunce

**Agustin Javier
Delgado Chala**
A jovial, angelic, sad
daughter
Dashed garage jovial
lunatic
Ageing Dracula, jovial
deaths

Rivaldo Ferreira
Evil, afraid error
Forever rid a liar

Alen Boksic
Lies on back
Lose in back
Likes bacon
I lack bones

**Hernn Evaristo
Medford Bryan**
Abhorred smart
over-fed ninny
Ever-fresh drab and
tiny moron

Ebbe Sand
Danes ebb
Bend base
Bed beans

Luis Figo
I foil Gus

Augustine Okocha
Caution! Huge oaks
Cook as a huge unit
Hooks cute iguana

Fabien Barthez
Fine zebra bath
Ban zebra thief
Fab in the zebra.

Paolo Maldini
I'm a piano doll
I'm a loo pan lid
An oil diploma

And finally, here is another retired football legend:

George Best
Go get beers

97

Crazy Games

Talk Like a Pundit

Pick any five of the sentences below, put them together and you'll be talking like a football expert. Try it and see!

It ain't over 'til the fat lady sings.
Records are made to be broken.
It's a game of two halves.
That's the key to the game.
There's no love lost between these two teams.
There are no easy games.
They have to stay focused.
They have to dig deep.
He makes it look easy.
He always gives 110 percent.
What an incredible turnaround.
We're taking it one game at a time.
They've been here before.
It's do or die.
They've got their backs against the wall.
He can make things happen out there.
He has a lot of potential.
He's got a great future ahead of him.
He's a great role model.
They're a dark horse team.

They're a team to be reckoned with.
This team travels well.
You have to respect . . .
They pride themselves on . . .
Football is a funny old game.
A game is not won until it is lost.
It's a nail biter.
The fans are getting their money's worth.
These two teams are fighting tooth and nail.
This game has gone true to form.
You can feel the electricity.
They're within striking distance now.
It's a whole new ball game.
That was a missed opportunity.
You can't teach that.
That was textbook
They're firing on all cylinders.
Crunch time.
This is just a walk in the park for them now.
They're blowing the game wide open.
That's gotta' hurt.
They have to get back into their offensive rhythm.
They'll have a lot to discuss at half-time.
They outplayed us . . .
We weren't mentally prepared.
We didn't get the job done.
My hat's off to them.
Give them all the credit.
The best team won today.
We can still hold our heads high.
We're in the business of winning.

THROW-IN

During a match against Kuwait in World Cup 1982 Giresse scored France's fourth goal while the Kuwaiti defenders did nothing. They claimed that they had stopped playing after hearing the referee's whistle. There was a big argument, and the Kuwaiti FA President, Prince Fahid, came on to the field to join in. Finally the Russian referee Miroslav Stupar disallowed the goal. France scored again anyway and FIFA later fined the Kuwaiti team £8,000 for Prince Fahid's interference!

More Referee Jokes

Why do referees die with their boots on?
Because they don't want to stub their toes when they kick the bucket!

A referee went outside in the pouring rain with no protection, but not a hair on his head got wet. How come?
He was bald.

How do you make a referee's eyes light up?
Shine a torch in his ear.

Why is a row of rabbits moving backwards the same as a referee's head?
They are both a receding hairline.

What does a referee call a rabbit sitting on his face?
Unwanted facial hare.

What's black and lies at the side of the pitch.
A dead referee.

What's black and green and lies at the side of the pitch.
A dead referee two months later.

What has eight legs, is green and black, and if it fell out of a tree would kill you?
Two referees and a pool table.

How do you make a referee burn his ear?
Ring him up while he is ironing!

Why did the referee pour a drink over his chest?
He wanted to wet his whistle.

Why did the referee cross the road?
Because the chicken was on holiday.

How do you keep a referee happy for hours?
Give him a piece of paper with PTO written on both sides.

Did you hear about the referee who tried to iron his curtains?
He fell out of the window.

What does a referee do if he splits his sides laughing?
Starts running until he gets a stitch.

Did you hear about the referee who was so keen on road safety that he always wore white at night?
Last winter he was knocked down by a snow plough.

What steps would a referee take if a player tried to hit him?
Great big ones!

What's the difference between an American referee and English referee?
About 3000 miles!

Referee: Doctor, Doctor. My wife thinks she's a clock!
Doctor: Well stop winding her up then!

Referee: Doctor, Doctor! I think I'm a dog!
Doctor: Sit down, please.
Referee: But I'm not allowed on the furniture!

A referee walked into a bar holding a dog poo in his hand. 'Look everyone,' he cried. *'See what I almost stood on!'*

What is brown, hairy, and wears a black shirt and shorts?
A coconut disguised as a referee.

102

What should a referee take if he is run down?
The number plate of the vehicle that hit him!

Did you hear about the referee who tried to cross the channel?
He couldn't find a long enough plank.

What goes whistle whoosh, whistle whoosh?
A referee caught in a revolving door.

Why did the referee run around his bed?
To catch up on his sleep!

Did you hear about the smelly referee who spent a fortune on deodorants before he found out that nobody liked him anyway?

A referee was having his hair cut and noticed that the hairdresser's hands were filthy. When he pointed this out the hairdresser replied, 'Yes, sir, no one has been in for a shampoo yet.'

What happened when the referee had a brain transplant?
The brain rejected him.

Did you hear about the referee who thought he was Dracula?
He was a pain in the neck.

103

Did you hear about the little referee who thought he was Dracula?
He was a pain in the backside.

Barber: How would you like your hair cut, sir?
Referee: In complete silence.

A referee went into the local department store where he saw a sign on the escalator — DOGS MUST BE CARRIED. The referee then spent the next two hours looking for a dog.

Referee: Doctor, doctor, I keep seeing double.
Doctor: Take a seat, please.
Referee: Which one?

Referee: Please call me a taxi.
Porter: OK, but you look more like a referee to me.

Did you hear about the referee who tried to swim the English Channel?
He had one mile to go, but got tired and decided to swim back.

How do referees dress on a cold day?
Quickly!

How can you make a tall referee short?
Borrow all his money.

THROW-IN

One of the most questionable managerial decisions was taken by Brazilian coach Ademar Pimenta in 1938. Although his star player Leonidas had scored six goals in the last two rounds, Pimenta decided to save him for the final. So Leonidas had to sit on the bench during the semi-final and watch his team get beaten 2-1 by Italy. He further proved his manager wrong during the bronze match by scoring two more goals!

Fantasy World Cup Squads

MEXICAN SQUAD FOR WORLD CUP 2002

Altitudo

Tequila   Hopelez   Tortilla   Vivazapata

Chihuahua   Siesta   Enchilada   Guadalajara

Jesus   Jesus

SUBS
Jesus Burrito Jesus Jesus

105

USA SQUAD FOR WORLD CUP 2002

Bud Lite

Brad　　　　Hank　　　　Tab　　　　George Junior

George Junior II　　　　George Junior III

Teddy　　　　Tiger　　　　Tom　　　　Elvis

SUBS
Nascar Rally
Duke Nukem

ITALIAN SQUAD FOR WORLD CUP 2002

De Niro

Pacino　　　　LeonardoDiCaprio　　　　Brando

Totti　　　　Botti　　　　Potti

Trevi　　　　Botticelli

Wobblijelli　　　　Spendapenni

SUBS
Michaelangelo

106

FRENCH SQUAD FOR WORLD CUP 2002

Voltaire

Fredastaire   Mediumrare

Le Creuset   Le Touquet   Henri   Ennui

Fromagefrais   Minibabibell   Yopplais   Danone

Ask the Anorak

Who are the World Cup Career Leading Scorers?

Name	Team	Years	Goals
Gerd Müller	West Germany	1970, 1974	14
Just Fontaine	France	1958	13
Pele	Brazil	1958, 1962, 1966, 1970	12
Sandor Kocsis	Hungary	1954	11
Jurgen Klinsmann	Germany	1990, 1994, 1998	11
Teofilo Cubillas	Peru	1970, 1978	10
Gregorz Lato	Poland	1974, 1978, 1982	10
Gary Lineker	England	1986, 1990	10
Helmut Rahn	West Germany	1954, 1958	10

Footy Earnometer

We all know that top footballers earn a fortune. It would easily take most families over a hundred years to earn what they earn in one. Doesn't it make you sick? There are always lots of rumours about which footballer earns the most. Nobody really knows just how much they earn because it's all based on their transfer fee and bonuses, and that's before you include advertising and sponsorship deals.

But it hasn't always been like this. In 1891 the maximum wage for a football player in England was legally set at £4 a month. The signing on fee was an amazing £10! In 1961 this maximum wage restriction was removed and Johnny Haynes of Fulham became the first British footballer to earn £100 a week.

OK, so sorry if your dad reckons these figures are out of date! But here are ten modern players and their salaries. Use the Earnometer opposite to see how much they earn per minute, then annoy everyone during a World Cup match by giving a running total! (e.g. multiply by 45 to work out what each player earns during the first half!). We've assumed that each player takes part in about 60 games per year.

Name	Team	Annual Salary	Per game	Per minute (incl 8 mins injury time)
Zinédine Zidane	France	£8 million	£130,000	£1,326
Raul Gonzalez	Spain	£6 million	£100,000	£1,020
Francesco Totti	Italy	£5.5 million	£91,000	£928
Luis Figo	Portugal	£5 million	£83,000	£846
Alvaro Recoba	Uruguay	£5 million	£83,000	£846
David Beckham	England	£4.2 million	£70,000	£714
Rivaldo	Brazil	£4 million	£67,000	£683
Roy Keane	Republic of Ireland	£4 million	£67,000	£683
Gabriel Batistuta	Argentina	£4 million	£67,000	£683
Alen Boksic	Croatia	£3.2 million	£53,000	£540

THROW-IN

It took José Batista just 56 seconds to get sent off for Uruguay against Scotland in the 1986 WC finals. He holds the record of the fastest sending off in the WC finals.

Own Goals

'If we played like that every week we wouldn't be so inconsistent.'

BRYAN ROBSON

'If I walked on water, my accusers would say it is because I can't swim.'

BERTI VOGTS

'What a goal by Reeves! That was straight from the top drawer – no, the wardrobe!'

NICK BARNES

'We probably got on better with the likes of Holland, Belgium, Norway and Sweden, some of whom are not even European.'

JACK CHARLTON

'To play Holland, you have to play the Dutch.'

RUUD GULLIT

'The World Cup is every four years, so it's going to be a perennial problem.'

GARY LINEKER

'We could've taken the lead before we even scored.'

PETER BEARDSLEY

'No team has ever scored a goal from the stand.'

ALAN HANSEN

110

THROW-IN

The Brazil–Hungary game in World Cup 1954 (Switzerland) was nicknamed 'The Battle of Berne' because it was so disgraceful. Three players were sent off and were still fighting as they left the pitch!

Even More Referee Jokes

When can a referee's pockets be empty and still have something in them?
When they are full of holes.

Referee: Excuse me, can I try on these shorts in the window?
Shop Assistant: Why don't you use the changing room like everyone else?

How can you tell an old referee from a young referee?
An old referee can sing and brush his teeth at the same time.

What's the difference between a referee with a toothache and a rainstorm?
One roars with pain, the other pours with rain.

111

What's green, has four legs and two whistles?
Two seasick referees.

How do you get a referee into the fridge?
1. Open door.
2. Insert referee.
3. Close door.

How do you get an elephant into the fridge?
1. Open door.
2. Remove referee.
3. Insert elephant.
4. Close door.

Did you hear about the referee whose fingernails were so long that when he picked his nose he scratched his brain?

Did you hear about the referee who plugged his electric blanket into the toaster by mistake? He spent the night popping in and out of bed.

What has two legs, a whistle and flies?
A dead referee.

Where does a referee leave his dog when he goes shopping?
In the barking lot.

112

What do you call a referee with an elephant on his head?
Squashed.

What's the difference between a referee and a biscuit?
You can't dip a referee in your tea.

Why did the referee have sponge cake in one ear and jelly in his other ear?
He was a trifle deaf.

What do you call a referee with a rabbit in his shorts?
Warren.

What do you call a referee with a lavatory on his head?
John.

Why did the referee shut his eyes when he looked in the mirror?
He wanted to see what he looked like when he was asleep.

What do you call a referee on his knees?
Neil.

THROW-IN

In the World Cup in 1978, Peruvian goalkeeper Ramon Quiroga was booked for a foul in the opponent's half of the field!

Crazy Games

World Cup Lottery Numbers

There's a lot of truth in the old saying: 'The referee was booking everyone. I thought he was filling in his lottery numbers.'

There's a great way you can watch the World Cup and choose your parent's lottery numbers at the same time.

Every time the referee awards a yellow card, make a note of the number of the player that he gives it to. Also, the number of the player on the other side who wins a free kick. Then multiply these two numbers together. If the result is smaller than fifty then circle that number on the grid opposite. If it is an even number greater than forty-nine, then divide by two until it is. If it is an odd number and greater than forty-nine, subtract one and then divide by two until it is smaller than fifty. Then circle the number below.

For example, if a number 7 is given a yellow card and number 9 is awarded a free kick, you must multiply 7 by 9 = 63. Because it is an odd number greater than forty-nine, you must subtract one and divide by two. 63−1=62 ÷ 2 = 31

114

When you have circled six numbers on the grid below,
you have chosen six lucky lottery numbers!

1	11	21	31	41
2	12	22	32	42
3	13	23	33	43
4	14	24	34	44
5	15	25	35	45
6	16	26	36	46
7	17	27	37	47
8	18	28	38	48
9	19	29	39	49
10	20	30	40	

THROW-IN

In Spain 1982, substitute Lazlo Kiss
of Hungary scored a hat-trick
against El Salvador. The final score
was 10–1, the biggest win in World
Cup history.

Goalkeeper Jokes

Why do goalkeepers paint their toenails pink?
So they can hide in cherry trees.

Have you ever seen a goalkeeper in a cherry tree?
Shows how effective their disguise is.

Why do digital watches make rotten goalkeepers?
Because they've got no hands.

Why did the goalkeeper dye his hair yellow?
To see if blondes really do have more fun.

Which goalkeepers can jump higher than the crossbar?
All of them – crossbars can't jump.

A goalkeeper who was down on his luck, saw a sign
outside a police station which read: MAN WANTED FOR
ROBBERY. So he went in and applied for the job!

Waiter, waiter, do you serve goalkeepers?
No sir, they won't fit in the microwave.

What happened to the goalkeeper who brushed his teeth
with gunpowder?
He kept shooting his mouth off.

116

Why did the goalkeeper hold his boot to his ear?
Because he liked sole music!

A seven-foot goalkeeper with round shoulders, very long arms and one leg ten inches shorter than the other walked into a clothes shop.
'I'd like to see a suit that will fit me,' he told the shop assistant.
'So would I, sir,' the shop assistant replied. 'So would I.'

What has a black shorts, a whistle and is found at the North Pole?
A goalkeeper with no sense of direction.

Why did the goalkeeper push his bed into the fireplace?
He wanted to sleep like a log.

One very hot day an extremely small referee went into a cafe, put his newspaper on a table and went to the counter. But on returning with a cup of tea he saw that his place had been taken by a huge, bearded, ferocious-looking 300-pound goalkeeper who was over seven feet tall.
'Excuse me,' said the referee to the goalkeeper, 'but you're sitting in my seat.'
'Oh yeah?' snarled the big goalkeeper. 'Prove it!'
'Certainly. You're sitting on my ice cream.'

What's the difference between a rabbit who goes jogging and an eccentric goalkeeper?
One is a fit bunny, the other is a bit funny.

What goalkeepers have the shortest legs?
The smallest ones.

What is the best day of the week for a goalkeeper to sleep?
Snooze-day!

Why did the goalkeeper stand on his head?
His feet were tired!

How do you make a goalkeeper cross?
Nail two goalkeepers together.

Where does a 300-pound goalkeeper sleep?
Anywhere he wants.

What position do ghosts play in soccer?
In ghoul.

Crazy Games

Crowd Spotting

This is another Bingo game, where you have to cross ten things off your scorecard, only this time you score by watching the crowd (forget about what's happening on the pitch!). You can start playing this before the match starts – when the TV camera is more likely to show the crowd.

Here are some examples, but you can think up lots of
your own:

picking nose
crying
wearing a silly hat
painted face
blowing something
eating
drinking

yawning
in fancy dress
shaking head
singing
laughing
with child on shoulders
looking bored

Own Goals

'He dribbles a lot and the opposition don't like it – you
can see it all over their faces.'

BIG RON

'I'd like to play for an Italian club, like Barcelona.'

MARK DRAPER

'Football's not just about scoring goals – it's about winning.'

ALAN SHEARER

'The opening ceremony was good, although I missed it.'

GRAEME LE SAUX

'Well, either side could win it, or it could be a draw.'

BIG RON

119

THROW-IN

German chemists have made a replica of the World Cup trophy that is the size of one molecule. That is less than 100-millionth the size of the original.

Crazy Games

World Cup Porsche Scam

Do you dream of being a professional footballer and being signed for Juventus for £20 million? Have you already decided which top-of-the-range sports car you are going to buy? Well, how's this for a great way to get over £18 million in just one month, without doing anything? It's legal, foolproof and very simple.

OK, but where's the catch? There isn't one (except maybe bankrupting your parents). Here's how.

On May 31, your dad will be in a really good mood because it is the first day of World Cup 2002. This is probably the best moment in four years to talk to him about pocket money. Tell him you have a business proposition that will mean that by the final on June 30, he will never have to pay you another penny again. (Sounds good.) All you ask is that he gives you one penny on Day 1 of the World Cup, 2 pence on Day 2, 4 pence on Day 3 and so on, doubling the pennies each day until the championship final on June 30. Tell him you're feeling generous and this is a once only, take-it-or-leave-it World Cup offer! Get him to sign the contract below and then start choosing cars!

I _____ being in sound mind and body, promise to pay _____ 1p pocket money on May 31 2002, 2p on June 1, 4p on June 2 and so on, doubling up each day until June 30. I understand that after this time I will never have to pay any pocket money again. Sounds like a great idea. Where do I sign?

Signed _____

Witnessed by (you) _____

Did you know that when you start doubling things up, small numbers can become enormous very quickly! On June 12, when England play Nigeria, your dad will have to

121

pay you £40.96 pocket money. But by the first semi-final on June 25, he will owe you £335,544.32, and your pocket money on the day of the final will be a staggering £10,737,418.24. Over the month he will have paid you over £21 million in total. And don't believe him when he says he can't pay up – ask him how much money he spent on beer!

THROW-IN

Only seven countries have won the World Cup: Brazil (58, 62, 70, 94), Italy (34, 38, 82), Germany (54, 74, 90), Uruguay (30, 50), Argentina (78, 86) England (66) and France (98).

An A-Z of World Cup Football

Aggregate
A small island off the coast of Scotland where Maths teachers who can't add up go to retire. There is one pub where they watch the World Cup and when the scores are announced, there's one score for us and another for them. That's why commentators say 'The score is one nil, and two-three on aggregate.'

Annette
A woman who stands behind the goalkeeper.

Attacking Team
What the Italian supporters do if they lose.

Bad haircut
Also called a mullet. Very popular in the 1970s and 1980s.
Now most players just dye it or shave it all off to show how
individual they are.

Blind side
The referee's right and left side. Also front and back.

Centre spot
When a player has a zit in between his eyebrows.

Change shirts
What Manchester United does five times a season.

Coach
Large slow thing with either four wheels or two legs and a
tracksuit.

Cones
Used by players in training to dribble around, but
sometimes the ice-cream falls on the floor in a big lump.

Corner
There are four of these on a football pitch, eight if you
count the top of David Seaman's head.

Dribbling
What football players are very good at when they're under
twenty and over eighty.

Early doors
The name for the first few minutes of an England match.
So named because the players look like large bits of wood
until they've relaxed into their game (except for Scotland,
who always play like planks).

Extra time
When the referee is wearing two wrist watches.

Free kick
Rare in football these days, since players get paid a fortune just to put their boots on.

Making space
Soccer games are won by taking advantage of space. Before a team can take advantage of space, it must first create the space. Stupid players are best at this, because they already have lots of space between their ears.

Obstruction
Anything that gets thrown onto the pitch which disrupts play. e.g. toilet paper, seats, smoke bombs, policeman's helmets.

One touch soccer
The style of football that Scotland play. They usually get one touch of the ball in each match.

Pass the ball
What you must do if you swallow the ball.

Playoffs
The closest England will ever get to another World Cup Final.

Rolls Royce
What members of the Saudi Arabian football team are given if they score a goal.

Running away from their mates
What players do when they have just scored a goal. What's wrong with a good hug? Ten years ago you couldn't prize celebrating team mates apart without a crow bar. Now all the players want to do when they've scored is duck and weave and take all the glory for themselves.

Sliding tackle
What footballers get when their underpants are too big.

Stadia
What the England team should have done, and saved themselves the cost of flying to Korea.

Stand
The part of the stadium where you are not allowed to stand.

Swim with concrete boots
What members of the Saudi Arabian football team are given if they don't score a goal.

Throw-in
Being sick in reverse.

Tie game
Experimenting with your neckwear. (See *David Beckham*)

Toilet paper
You may be mistaken for thinking that fans sometimes throw toilet paper on the pitch, but in fact these are till rolls thrown by spectators sitting in corporate hospitality when they realize how much they are being charged for a ham sandwich and a paperweight.

Turning your opponent
When you persuade your opponent to join your team.

Volley
An Irish valley

THROW-IN

Italian goalkeeper Walter Zenga holds the record of longest unbeaten run in World Cup history. He played 517 minutes (Almost 6 games) without conceding a goal in the 1990 tournament.

125

Injury Time

Why did a footballer take a piece of rope onto the pitch?
He was the skipper!

What lights up a football stadium?
A football match!

A referee arrives at the gates of heaven, where Saint Peter welcomes him and says, 'Before I can let you in, I must ask you what you have done in your life that was particularly good.'
The referee thinks for a few minutes and then admits to Saint Peter that he hasn't done anything particularly good in his life.
'Well,' says Saint Peter, 'have you done anything particularly brave in your life?'
'Yes, I have,' replies the referee proudly.
So the referee explains, 'I was refereeing the World Cup final between Italy and Korea. The score was nil-nil and there was only one more minute of play to go in the second half when I awarded a penalty against Korea.'
'Yes,' responded Saint Peter, 'I agree that was a real act of bravery. Can you perhaps tell me when this took place?'
'Certainly,' the referee replied, 'about three minutes ago.'

THROW-IN

In 1984, after Mike Bagley of Bristol was booked for swearing, he took the referee's notebook, ripped out and ate the page with his name on it!

Final Whistle

David Beckham was driving along when a lorry driver made him pull over. The lorry driver draws a circle with a piece of chalk and says, 'Stand in that ring while I smash your car up.' 'OK' says Becks.

So the man kicks in the lights, and David starts to giggle. Then the lorry driver smashes the windscreen, and David starts laughing. Finally he backs over it with his lorry. By now David is in hysterics, so the lorry driver says 'What's so funny? I've just wrecked your car.'

David replies 'Ah ha! But what you didn't know is that every time you turned your back, I took my foot out of the circle.'

Why did the spaceship land outside Sol Campbell's bedroom?
He left the landing light on.

127

Why did David Beckham take a car door with him to Korea?
So that if it got too hot he could wind down the window.

How do you join the England World Cup squad?
With a tube of superglue.

Why are soccer matches very windy?
Because of all the fans.

At a World Cup fixture a man tries get in the ground with a gorilla.
'Excuse me, Sir', said a policeman, 'I saw you with him yesterday and advized you to take him to the zoo.'
'Yes, I did as you said' replied the man, 'and then we went to the cinema and a restaurant, so today I thought he might like to see some football.'

Mother: Where did you get that ball?
Boy: We found it
Mother: Are you sure it was lost?
Boy: Yes, we saw people looking for it.

What has 22 legs and goes, 'Crunch, crunch, crunch?'
A football team eating crisps.